YOU CHOOSE
BOOKS™

THE SALEM WITCH TRIALS

An Interactive History Adventure

by Matt Doeden

Consultant:
Walter W. Woodward, PhD
Associate Professor of History and
Connecticut State Historian
University of Connecticut
Storrs, Connecticut

PSTONE PRESS
a capstone imprint

You Choose Books are published by Capstone Press,
151 Good Counsel Drive, P.O. Box 669, Mankato, Minnesota 56002.
www.capstonepub.com

Books published by Capstone Press are manufactured with paper
containing at least 10 percent post-consumer waste.

Library of Congress Cataloging-in-Publication Data
Doeden, Matt.
 The Salem witch trials : an interactive history adventure / by Matt Doeden.
  p. cm. — (You choose history)
 Includes bibliographical references and index.
 Summary: "Describes the people and events involved in the Salem witch trials. The reader's
choices reveal the historical details from the perspectives of an accused witch, the family member
of an accused witch, and an accuser"—Provided by publisher.
 ISBN 978-1-4296-5478-4 (library binding) — ISBN 978-1-4296-6272-7 (paperback)
 1. Trials (Witchcraft)—Massachusetts—Salem—History—17th century—Juvenile literature.
2. Witchcraft—Massachusetts—Salem—History—17th century—Juvenile literature. 3. Salem
(Mass.)—History—Colonial period, ca. 1600-1775—Juvenile literature. I. Title.
 KFM2478.8.W5D64 2011
 133.4'3097445—dc22   2010035014

Editorial Credits
Angie Kaelberer, editor; Bobbie Nuytten, designer; Wanda Winch, media researcher;
   Eric Manske, production specialist

Image Credits
Alamy: North Wind Picture Archives, 6, 39; The Bridgeman Art Library International:
Collection of the New York Historical Society, USA, Thomas Satterwhite Noble, cover, ©Look
and Learn/Private Collection, 45, Massachusetts Historical Society, Boston, Mass., USA,
83, Private Collection/Howard Pyle, 46; Corbis: Baldwin H. Ward & Kathryn C. Ward, 11,
Bettmann, 85, 100; Getty Images Inc.: George Eastman House/Briggs Co., 96; The Granger
Collection, 76; Mary Evans Picture Library, 99; North Wind Picture Archives, 12, 29, 33, 57,
65, 73, 88; SuperStock Inc./SuperStock, 21

Printed in the United States of America in Stevens Point, Wisconsin.
112014   008623R

TABLE OF CONTENTS

ABOUT YOUR ADVENTURE

YOU are living in the Massachusetts Colony during the late 1600s. The colony is filled with deeply religious colonists who struggle to survive. Just the mention of witchcraft causes panic.

In this book you'll explore how the choices people made meant the difference between life and death. The events you'll experience happened to real people.

Chapter One sets the scene. Then you choose which path to read. Follow the directions at the bottom of each page. The choices you make will change your outcome. After you finish one path, go back and read the others for new perspectives and more adventures.

YOU CHOOSE the path
you take through history.

Puritans dressed simply and believed in lives filled with work and prayer.

A TIME OF FEAR

Life in the colony of Massachusetts in 1692 was little like life today. The colony was small. Its population was scattered. People were in constant danger. Crop failure, disease, harsh winters, and wars with American Indians made life difficult.

Christianity was at the heart of every community. Massachusetts had many Puritans. Puritans were very strict in their Christian beliefs. They believed that God and the devil played active roles in their lives. Good fortune was a blessing from God. Bad fortune often was considered the work of the devil. To the Puritans, the devil often tried to make people question their faith.

Turn the page.

The Puritans believed that some people struck deals with the devil. In exchange for doing evil, the devil gave them powers. These people were called witches. Puritans believed witches' actions could destroy good Christian people and communities. Many said there was only one way to deal with a witch. A convicted witch had to die.

The Puritans had long believed in witches. But in 1692 everything changed. For reasons that even today are not fully clear, 1692 marked the beginning of a widespread witch hunt. The accusations were centered in the village of Salem. Two Salem girls, Betty Parris and Abigail Williams, began to accuse others in the village of using the devil's powers to torment them. Many people were arrested and put on trial.

VICTIMS OF THE SALEM WITCH TRIALS, 1692*

Name	Date Executed
Bridget Bishop	June 10
George Burroughs	August 19
Martha Carrier	August 19
Giles Corey	September 19
Martha Corey	September 22
Mary Eastey	September 22
Sarah Good	July 19
Elizabeth How	July 19
George Jacobs Sr.	August 19
Susannah Martin	July 19
Rebecca Nurse	July 19
Alice Parker	September 22
Mary Parker	September 22
John Proctor	August 19
Ann Pudeater	September 22
Wilmott Reed	September 22
Margaret Scott	September 22
Samuel Wardwell	September 22
Sarah Wilds	July 19
John Willard	August 19

*From four to 17 other accused witches died in prison.

Turn the page.

Salem was the most famous Massachusetts village to round up accused witches. But it wasn't the only one. Over the next year, fear of witchcraft grew. Neighbors accused neighbors. Family members desperately tried to prove the innocence of their loved ones. Clergymen, community leaders, and court officers called magistrates struggled to understand what was happening.

Life in Salem and other Puritan villages during this time was difficult. For the accused, their lives and reputations hung in the balance. Accusers had to worry about the consequences of their actions. How people viewed the events taking place would have depended largely on their situation. Were they accused? Was a friend or family member accused? Or did they believe that someone else might be a witch?

People turned on their friends and neighbors, accusing them of practicing witchcraft.

How will you choose to experience this time in history?

❧ To be a young woman defending herself against accusations of witchcraft, turn to page **13**.

❧ To be the son of an accused woman, turn to page **47**.

❧ To accuse someone of being a witch, turn to page **77**.

Church was an important part of Puritan life. Everyone was expected to regularly attend services.

CHAPTER 2

FALSELY ACCUSED

It's 1692. The sun shines on the snow-covered ground. Your family and neighbors walk together into the village of Salem. Even though you are going to church, the men carry muskets. You trust them to protect you from bears, Indians, or anything else that might threaten you.

You catch the gaze of your neighbor Susanna. At age 15, Susanna is just a year younger than you, but you're not friends. You think Susanna is rude and selfish. She doesn't like you either. She sneers at you and turns away.

Turn the page.

The church is filled with people. As the Reverend Samuel Parris leads the service, everyone looks concerned. The events of the past few weeks have been hard to understand.

The accusations started with two young girls, Betty Parris and Abigail Williams. The two girls began acting oddly. They screamed and spoke words no one could understand. Their bodies twisted into uncomfortable positions.

The girls believed their behavior was caused by witchcraft and accused three women of casting spells on them. Two, Sarah Good and Sarah Osborne, are Puritan women. The other is a slave woman named Tituba.

Now more and more people are accusing their neighbors of witchcraft. It all makes little sense to you. You know most of the people who are accused. It's hard to believe they would make a deal with the devil.

After church you notice Susanna talking to the Reverend Parris' 9-year-old daughter, Betty. She is one of the girls who have accused people of witchcraft. Betty and Susanna then rush up to the minister and begin talking to him. At one point, Susanna turns and points at you. You shiver with fear. What are they telling him?

You turn to leave, but the minister and several other men are coming your way. Your father sees this and moves between you and the men.

Turn the page.

"Step aside," Constable Joseph Herrick tells your father.

"What is this?" Father asks.

"Your daughter stands accused of witchcraft. We must take her in for questioning."

"You'll take this girl over my dead body!" Father shouts. You know that he will fight for you, but you don't want to see him hurt.

➤ *To give yourself up, go to page* **17**.

➤ *To run, turn to page* **20**.

Father shoves one of the men, knocking him to the ground. But others quickly grab Father and hold him back.

"Stop!" you shout. "I will go with you. Let my father go!"

"No! Don't!" Father yells, but it's too late. The men are leading you away to be questioned.

"This is in God's hands now," Parris tells Father as you're taken to a nearby inn. "If your daughter is innocent, he will save her."

Turn the page.

At the inn John Hathorne, a magistrate, begins to question you. "Did you make a deal with the devil?" he asks. The Reverend Parris listens at his side.

"No! Of course not!" you answer.

"Susanna tells us she has seen you sticking pins into small dolls. She says you sometimes speak in a strange language. She has seen you with the slave woman Tituba, a confessed witch. Susanna says you appear at her bedside at night and torment her. Why do you do these things?"

You insist that none of it is true. You try to explain that Susanna doesn't like you and never has. But Hathorne just keeps asking questions.

"Was it Sarah Good who turned you from God? Tell us, child. You might still be saved. But we must know."

Sarah Good is one of the other women who is accused of witchcraft. She is poor and she and her young daughter often have to beg for food. Also, she and her husband do not attend church services regularly.

Good is a bit of a village outcast, but you have no reason to believe that she is a witch. And she has never approached you. But it seems certain that she'll be found guilty. Blaming her could give you a chance to live.

➤ To agree that Sarah Good turned you toward witchcraft, turn to page **23**.

➤ To tell the truth, turn to page **26**.

As your father throws a punch at one of the men, you turn and dart in the opposite direction. You run out of the church's door and toward a patch of woods. As you run, you trip on the hem of your dress, twisting your right ankle. You try to get up and limp away, but you're soon caught.

Several men lead you to a small inn in Salem. Inside the inn, other men restrain your father. You sit down, and a man approaches you. He introduces himself as magistrate John Hathorne.

"Why have you made a deal with the devil?" Hathorne asks.

"What? I ... I never ... it's a lie!" you stammer. Your fear makes it difficult to speak.

"You ran from us. Why would an innocent woman run? Tell us, did Sarah Good turn you to witchcraft?

People were unable to keep their family members from being arrested and questioned about witchcraft.

Turn the page.

"Nonsense," your father shouts. "That woman hasn't had anything to do with my daughter. Now let her go!"

Constable Herrick leads your father outside. Only you, Hathorne, and the Reverend Parris remain in the room. Parris stares at you. "If you are truly innocent, you will be able to recite the Lord's Prayer. No witch serving the devil can perform such a feat. Stand and say the prayer and we may believe you."

You're so afraid that you're not sure you could say your own full name right now, much less the Lord's Prayer.

➤ To try to say the prayer, turn to page **28**.

➤ To refuse, turn to page **31**.

You take a deep breath and bury your face in your hands. "Yes," you whisper.

"Speak up. What did you just say?"

With tears in your eyes, you look up at him. You admit that Sarah Good introduced you to witchcraft.

"So it's true," Parris says sternly. "You have sinned against God, but I can see that you are sorry. You must testify at Sarah Good's trial. Tell the judge what you have said today, and you may be spared."

You wipe away tears and stand, thinking of Sarah. "Forgive me," you whisper.

Parris hears this. Misunderstanding your meaning, he looks you in the eye. "It is God whose forgiveness you should be seeking, not mine," he says.

Turn the page.

You're allowed to return home. Your parents know that the charges against you aren't true, but they're afraid of what is going to happen to you. Every morning you wake up filled with dread. Your fear increases in early June when Bridget Bishop is the first accused witch to be found guilty. She is hanged on June 10.

About two weeks later, you are brought to Sarah Good's trial. You watch as witnesses take the stand against Good. Even her husband and 4-year-old daughter testify against her.

You are angered by what you see. At one point, Good's accusers writhe in pain. They say that she is still attacking them. The judge glares at Good. "Why do you hurt these children?" he demands.

"I do not hurt them," she answers. "I am falsely accused."

You are the last witness to testify. First the magistrate asks your name, age, and other basic questions. Then comes the question you have been dreading. "Is it true that Sarah Good turned you toward witchcraft?"

You hesitate and glance at Good. She looks defeated. Your testimony won't make any difference. You know they'll hang her. But lying is wrong.

➺ *To lie, turn to page* **34**.

➺ *To tell the truth, turn to page* **36**.

Lying isn't the way to save yourself. "No, I have never practiced witchcraft. I have never even spoken to Sarah Good."

Hathorne stands close. "You don't have to protect her. We know Sarah Good has made a deal with the devil. Just admit to us that she drew you in. We can still help you if you tell the truth."

"But I'm telling the truth," you insist.

They don't believe you. You are charged with witchcraft and put in the jail of the nearby town of Ipswich. Over the next several days, accusations continue to fly. Respected members of the Salem community are being named as witches. Women, men, and even children have been charged. The jails are filling up.

Finally, the day of your trial comes. Early one morning you board a wagon headed to Salem. But along the way, one of the wagon wheels breaks down. The men in charge of you are busy fixing it. Nobody is watching you. A thick forest lies to the side of the road. If you ran, you might be able to slip away.

➻ To stay and face your trial, turn to page **33**.

➻ To run, turn to page **38**.

Carefully, you stand. You try to swallow, but your mouth is completely dry. You clutch your hands tightly to your body to keep them from shaking.

"Our Father," you whisper.

"Speak up!" Parris insists.

You take a deep, shaky breath and start again. Your heart is racing. You have never been this nervous.

"Our Father," you repeat. But your terrified mind goes blank. Your hands tremble. You can hear your pulse thundering inside your temples. You close your eyes and try to calm yourself.

"Enough of this," Hathorne says. "She can't get past the first line. Clearly the devil has a hold on this young woman."

Colonial jails were bleak places.

You are sent to a jail in the nearby town of Ipswich. You are not alone there. The jails are filling up as the accusations continue. The jails are cold and damp, and the sick and the healthy are crammed in together. Some people die before they ever reach trial.

Turn the page.

When the day of your trial comes, you are loaded into a wagon bound for Salem. But a few miles from Salem, one of the wagon wheels breaks.

As the men in charge of you fix the wheel, you are left unattended. If you wanted to, you could slip out the other side and escape into the woods. You're not sure what you would do then, but at least you wouldn't be headed to a courtroom.

➻ *To stay and face your trial, turn to page* **33**.

➻ *To make a run for it, turn to page* **38**.

There's no chance you'll be able to recite the Lord's Prayer right now. If you try, you'll never get through it. That will just make you look guilty. You drop your head into your hands and sob. You feel so powerless. Nothing you say will convince these men of your innocence.

You are taken to a jail in the nearby town of Ipswich. Weeks later you return to Salem to stand trial. Magistrates and judges watch you closely as you enter the courthouse. As you look around the room, you see few friendly faces. Your father reaches out and puts a hand on your shoulder, trying to reassure you. But you can see in his eyes that he has little hope. The village is against you.

Finally the trial begins. Hathorne demands to know why you are dealing with the devil.

Turn the page.

"I am not. I am a Christian. I pray to God that he will prove my innocence."

"The Reverend Parris asked you to recite the Lord's Prayer, and you refused. Is that true?"

"It is," you say. "I was scared and trembling. I was in no state to recite anything."

"So you say," Hathorne says. He begins to ask another question. You realize you have an opportunity here.

→ To interrupt the magistrate and offer to recite the prayer, turn to page **40**.

→ To move on to the next question, turn to page **42**.

Running won't solve anything. The only chance you have to get your life back is to prove your innocence in court. You wait in silence as the wagon wheel is repaired and you return to Salem.

The village is abuzz with excitement over the trials. You sense that few in the crowd are on your side. You hope the judges will be fairer.

Curious onlookers crowded into the courtrooms during the trials.

Turn to page 44.

You take a deep breath. "Yes, Sarah Good turned me to witchcraft," you lie. "I was arrested just in time, before I made a deal with the devil. I have prayed to God for forgiveness and left the evil ways behind."

As you speak, you see disgust in the eyes of many people in the courtroom. You know some of them will never look at you the same way again. But what choice did you have? Your own life was at risk, and Good was going to be found guilty either way.

Good is found guilty of witchcraft and sentenced to hang July 19. You and your father go to witness it. "You did what you had to do," your father explains. "But you must live with the consequences of your choices. This woman will die in part because of what you said."

You nod. "I understand," you say softly.

You watch as Good steps to the gallows. A rope is fitted around her neck. When Good is dropped from the gallows, the snapping rope breaks her neck, killing her. When it is over, your father takes your hand and leads you away. You'll never forget the look in Sarah Good's eyes. You were partly responsible for her death. You will live with that for the rest of your life.

35

THE END

To follow another path, turn to page 11.
To read the conclusion, turn to page 101.

As you open your mouth to answer the magistrate, you realize that you cannot go through with it. "No, it's not true," you say.

Hathorne pauses. Anger flashes in his eyes.

"None of it is true," you continue. "I never practiced witchcraft. Sarah Good never taught me anything. I was falsely accused and then pressured into testifying here."

The Reverend Parris stands up and points at you. "The devil is making her say these things! She is lying to protect her fellow witch!"

The crowd is in a state of confusion. You are taken to a jail cell. You wait there as the trial finishes. Later you learn that Good has been found guilty and sentenced to hang. Your honesty made no difference.

Weeks later you are led before a grand jury. Magistrates argue that your defense of Good is proof that you were working with her. But they have no real evidence. No one from the community testifies against you.

You are lucky. The grand jury returns a verdict of ignoramus. This means that the jurors didn't think there was enough evidence to prosecute you. It's not the same as being declared not guilty, but it means you're free to return to your life. You can't wait to put the dark days of the Salem witch trials behind you.

THE END

To follow another path, turn to page 11.
To read the conclusion, turn to page 101.

You leap from the wagon. You dart into the woods and keep running. From behind, you hear voices. Are the men after you?

You keep running. The hem of your dress tears on a tree branch. Another branch whacks you across the face. The voices behind you are fading.

You run deeper and deeper into the wilderness until you can't run anymore. You stop and fall to your knees. You realize that you're alone in the woods. There could be bears, wolves, or Indians at any turn.

The officials will find you if you go home. The only plan you can think of is to head for the city of Boston, about 15 miles from Salem. You might find work as a maid or a seamstress there. Even living on the streets would be better than death by hanging. You're not sure what is in store for you, but you know that life will never be the same.

Some accused people tried to escape before they were brought to trial.

THE END

To follow another path, turn to page 11.
To read the conclusion, turn to page 101.

"Wait," you say. "I can do it now. I will recite the prayer before everyone here."

"Very well," Hathorne agrees.

You take a deep breath and begin. You say the words you've known since childhood. You recite the prayer flawlessly. "She's innocent!" shouts someone from the back of the room.

You can see it in their faces. Even Hathorne looks convinced that you're not a witch. But just then screams fill the room.

"Make her stop, make her stop! Her spirit is attacking me!" It is Susanna. She is crying, screaming, and writhing on the ground. Just like that, everything you have done has been erased. You aren't surprised when the judges return a guilty verdict.

You almost proved your innocence. But people are fearful and superstitious. Witches are an easy scapegoat for anything that goes wrong. You know that you will be hanged for a crime you never committed. You only hope that the townspeople will soon come to their senses and that no more innocent people will die.

THE END

To follow another path, turn to page 11.
To read the conclusion, turn to page 101.

You can't find the courage to interrupt the magistrate. He asks you questions about the devil, about your accuser Susanna, and much more. Later, others testify against you. The Reverend Parris testifies that he believes Sarah Good has turned you toward witchcraft and that you're protecting her.

Susanna testifies next. She claims that she saw you change into a cat and then back into yourself again. She also says that a spirit that looks like you pinches her while she sleeps. As she leaves the stand, she glances at you with the hint of a smile on her lips.

You are found guilty and sentenced to death by hanging. Several days later, you are led to the gallows, along with one man and two other women convicted of witchcraft. One woman cries and begs for her life. But you remain silent. Begging will change nothing. You will at least die with your dignity.

As the rope is fitted around your neck, you close your eyes and think of your family. You know they never doubted your innocence. That is what you focus on during the last moments of your life.

43

THE END

To follow another path, turn to page 11.
To read the conclusion, turn to page 101.

The small courtroom is packed. Everyone stares as you walk to the stand. Magistrate Hathorne asks you many questions. You know that he is trying to trick you into admitting witchcraft. But you don't fall into his traps. You're sure the truth will save you.

"I am no witch," you tell him. "I pray to God every day. I pray that he will help you see the truth and find me innocent."

You see that your words are having an effect on the judges. But just then, Susanna stands up and points at you. "I see the devil!" she shouts. "He is standing right behind her, telling her what to say!"

People gasp in horror. The judges look at you with hatred. Tears stream down your face as you are pronounced guilty.

You will be hanged for a crime you never committed. You are just one of many innocent victims of the Salem witch trials.

During trials witnesses would often tell wild tales about demons and monsters.

THE END

To follow another path, turn to page 11.
To read the conclusion, turn to page 101.

Magistrates questioned accused witches to determine if there was enough evidence for indictment.

CHAPTER 3

A WITCH IN THE FAMILY?

It is a cool day early in the spring of 1692. You are outside tending to your family's chickens. At 16, you have taken on most of the farmwork since your father's death several months ago.

You do all you can to help your mother and younger siblings get by. James, your brother, is only 5, so he isn't able to help with the harder work. Your 11-year-old sister, Margaret, has frequent seizures, so she stays inside most of the time.

Turn the page.

Your family lives outside a Massachusetts village of a few hundred Puritans. Like you, most townspeople are honest, hardworking Christians. You like the village and the people. You even have plans to begin courting one of the neighbor girls, Abigail.

You hear the sound of horses approaching. You walk to the front of the house to see who it is. You are surprised to see the village constable, Abraham Lewis, riding alongside the Reverend Thomas Jacobs. The men do not call out in greeting or even wave. This worries you.

The men get off their horses. "We are here to speak with your mother," they tell you. You feel a wave of dread rising within you. You have heard about the recent events in Salem and across the colony. People everywhere are talking about witchcraft. Men and women are being hanged for dealing with the devil.

You can't be sure this visit has anything to do with witchcraft. Your mind races, trying to come up with another reason these two men are here. But nothing else makes sense. It's true that your family has missed church often in recent months, but that was because of your father's illness.

"Son, did you hear us?" says Constable Lewis. You've known and trusted this man all your life. But now he seems unfriendly.

"What is this about?" you ask.

"That is not your concern," the constable answers. "Now go fetch your mother."

➤ To go get your mother, turn to page **50**.

➤ To lie and say your mother isn't home, turn to page **51**.

"Wait here," you tell the men as you rush inside to get your mother. "The Reverend Jacobs and Constable Lewis are here," you tell her. "They want to see you."

The two of you walk outside. Jacobs and Lewis do not smile or greet your mother.

"Good sirs," Mother says. "How can I help you?"

"You stand accused of witchcraft," Jacobs says. "We need to bring you in for questioning."

"What?" Mother cries. "On what grounds?"

"We'll explain everything when we get to town," the constable replies.

Mother closes her eyes and nods slowly. "Look after your brother and sister," she tells you.

Turn to page 56.

"Mother isn't home," you say.

The Reverend Jacobs looks at you sharply. Clearly, he doesn't believe you. The two men glance at each other, then step around you, toward the house.

"She went … to Boston," you say, trying to keep yourself between the men and the house. You reach out your arms to block their way. Constable Lewis places a hand firmly on your shoulder and moves you aside.

"Lying is a sin, boy," says Jacobs. "Don't make things worse."

Lewis pounds on the door. You hear your mother's footsteps as she approaches. When she opens the door, you want to shout a warning to her. But it won't help.

"What is this about?" Mother asks.

Turn the page.

"Goodwife, you are accused of witchcraft," says Constable Lewis. "You will come with us for questioning. If we find cause to believe the accusations, you will be held in jail until you stand trial."

"This is ridiculous!" your mother shouts. "I'm not coming with you!"

"This is not a choice," the constable says. "Please do not make this more difficult than it already is."

Stunned, your mother steps out of the house. "Look after the children," she tells you. "I will clear this up and be home shortly."

Your father's musket sits just inside the door, easily within reach. You could grab for it and prevent these men from taking your mother.

➛ To grab the gun, go to page **53**.

➛ To do as your mother says, turn to page **56**.

You're not about to let these men arrest your mother for no good reason. You dart inside and grab the musket. You run back outside. "Stop!" you yell as you point the musket at the men.

"No!" your mother hisses at you. "Put that away. Now!"

"Listen to your mother, boy," the Reverend Jacobs orders.

As you glare at Jacobs, Constable Lewis rushes at you. He knocks you to the ground and grabs the musket.

"The boy lied to us," Jacobs says. "He drew his weapon on us. He is working with his mother. He will have to come along."

Turn the page.

With a shock, you realize that you also are being accused of witchcraft! The minister and the constable take you both into town for questioning. You learn that your mother is accused of bringing illness to both the people and animals of the village and nearby farms. Many people believe she is spreading evil. They say your father's death and Margaret's seizures are punishment for your mother's evil ways.

The constable puts both you and your mother in jail. You protest, but he tells you that you will have a chance to prove your innocence in court. The colony's governor has set up a special court just for witchcraft cases. Margaret and James are left to fend for themselves. You hear that a few neighbors are bringing them food.

The day before the trial is set to begin, a magistrate comes to speak to you. He makes you an offer. If you are willing to testify that your mother is a witch, the court will spare you.

Your mother's jail cell is next to yours. That night, you whisper to her, "Mother, they want me to testify against you to save myself. I can't do that."

Mother is silent for a few seconds. "You must do as they tell you," she replies sadly. "If we're both hanged, there will be no one to take care of your brother and sister."

→ To agree to the deal, turn to page **68**.

→ To refuse to testify against your mother, turn to page **71**.

You watch in fear as the two men lead Mother to town. You hope they'll discover that this is a mistake. But you're not so sure. Mother has always been willing to speak her mind, even when her ideas were unpopular. Many people object to a woman being so outspoken. That, combined with your father's illness and Margaret's seizures, will work against her.

You wish the Reverend Thomas Richards was still here. He was the minister here until three years ago, when he moved to another village. He was a good friend to your family and had some powerful connections. He might have been able to help.

The minister lives only a few hours' ride away. You could visit him and ask for his help. But there's no guarantee he'd even be willing to get involved. Or you could speak to Constable Lewis. He knows your family well. Maybe he would listen to reason.

Clergymen (right) were among the most respected people in colonial villages.

→ To seek out the Reverend Richards, turn to page 58.

→ To talk to Constable Lewis, turn to page 61.

The Reverend Richards is your best hope. You tell Margaret to look after James. Then you saddle your horse and ride briskly through the Massachusetts countryside. The colony is sparsely populated, and you have to watch for wild animal or Indian attacks.

Soon you reach the minister's village. You find him at the town's small church. He rushes out to greet you.

"Welcome!" he says. "I haven't seen you in years! What brings you so far from home?"

You tell him about your mother's arrest.

"That's ridiculous," he says. "Your mother is no witch. We must speak to the Reverend Jacobs immediately."

The two of you ride to the village and head straight for the jail. Your mother is being held there awaiting her trial. The Reverend Jacobs is speaking with Constable Lewis outside. The Reverend Richards joins them.

"I must speak with you privately," Richards tells Jacobs. The two ministers walk off together to discuss your mother's fate. You ask Lewis if you can speak to your mother, but he says it's not allowed.

Richards and Jacobs return about a half hour later. Richards takes you aside. "This is not good," he confides. "The Reverend Jacobs has several witnesses against your mother. The death of your father and your sister's condition will reflect poorly on her defense."

Turn the page.

"What can we do?" you ask.

"I can stay here and testify at the trial," Richards says. "Many people in this village know and trust me. My testimony might be enough. Or I can travel to Boston. As you know, Governor William Phips is a distant cousin of mine. I might be able to get him to help. But there's no guarantee I'll even be able to see him."

➤ To ask the Reverend Richards to stay as a witness, turn to page **63**.

➤ To ask him to get the governor's help, turn to page **66**.

You'll speak to Constable Lewis. He knows your family well. You hope he can clear up this misunderstanding.

Lewis is at the town jail. He tells you that a magistrate is questioning your mother about the case. "Surely you know these charges aren't true," you say.

"I don't know what to believe" he replies. "The Reverend Jacobs thinks it's true, and he's a man of God. And some strange things have happened to your family."

"But you've known my mother all your life!" you gasp.

"Go home," he continues. "If your mother is innocent, she can prove it in court." Discouraged, you leave.

Turn the page.

A few weeks later, your mother's trial begins. A panel of three judges, specially appointed by the governor, hears the case. Your mother's accusers say that she has brought illness to the village's people and farm animals. They also blame her for recent crop failures. Witnesses testify that your family has been absent from church recently. At one point, you see Abigail in the courtroom. She refuses to look at you.

It is too much to take. You stand up and shout. "It's lies! It's all lies!" Constable Lewis grabs you by the arms and hauls you out of the courtroom. "I'm sorry," he says. You spit at his feet.

Your mother is found guilty. She will hang for a crime she did not commit.

Turn to page 74.

"I'm sure your testimony would make the difference," you say. For the first time, you feel as if your mother might have a real chance.

On the day of the trial, you leave James and Margaret at home and travel with the Reverend Richards to the courthouse. The small building is packed with people. Three judges will hear the testimony. Several people approach you. "May God protect your mother," they say. You know that having the Reverend Richards at your side is a big help. The people here still trust him. He has had many of them sign a petition that says your mother is of the highest moral character.

At last, the trial begins. A magistrate lays out the case against your mother. She is a witch, he says, and she is causing disease and crop failure in the area. The Reverend Richards takes the stand and tries to appeal to reason.

Turn the page.

"I have known this woman for years. She is a good Christian. The charges against her are false."

"How long has it been since you lived here, Reverend?" the magistrate asks.

"Three years," Richards replies.

"And in those three years, how many times have you spoken to the accused?"

Richards pauses. "None."

The courtroom is silent. "So your testimony is that the accused was a good Christian three years ago, then?"

Richards looks down. "Yes."

The trial goes on. Your mother takes the stand, but she appears nervous and has trouble speaking. She can't defend herself against the accusations.

"I'm so sorry," Richards tells you. You both know what is coming. Your mother is found guilty of witchcraft and sentenced to hang. You weren't able to save her.

Accused witches were often convicted on the testimony of others.

Turn to page **74**.

"If you talk to the governor, maybe he could help," you tell Richards.

"I agree," the minister says. "I will do all that I can."

He leaves that day. All you can do is wait. More than a week passes without any word. Your hopes fade as the morning of the trial arrives.

You leave James and Margaret at home and head for the courthouse. It is packed. Few people will meet your eyes as you walk in.

Just as the trial is about to begin, the Reverend Richards enters the room. He rushes to the small table where the three judges sit. He shows them a piece of paper. The judges look at it carefully. The gathered crowd sits in curious silence as the judges call the magistrates up to the tables.

Finally, the group nods in agreement. One of the judges stands. "This is an order from Governor Phips," he announces. "All trials for witchcraft are suspended until further notice. The accused will return to jail until trials are resumed."

You breathe a sigh of relief. Tears stream down your mother's face.

"You know that this isn't over yet," Richards tells you. "Your mother can still be tried."

"I know," you reply. "But maybe the governor will realize what madness this is and stop the trials for good. At least we have some more time."

THE END

To follow another path, turn to page 11.
To read the conclusion, turn to page 101.

The next morning your heart is heavy as you tell the magistrate that you will testify against your mother.

"Good decision," he replies. "Defending a witch in court would have been unwise."

The trial begins the next day. Three judges sit at a small table as you and Mother are brought in. Many of the people from the village are there. Some of them look at you with fear and distrust. Others wish you well.

Mother's expression remains gloomy. She seems to have aged 10 years in the past few days. She nods at you. You know she still wants you to save yourself.

A magistrate tells the court about your father's long illness and your sister's strange condition. Several witnesses take the stand, including the Reverend Jacobs. "She and her family have stopped coming to church," he says. Other people speak about how their farm animals died and crops failed after your mother passed by their farms. Some even say that a spirit that looked like your mother terrorized their children at night.

Finally, it's your turn. Mother closes her eyes as you take the stand. You don't know if you can go through with this.

"Is your mother a witch?" the magistrate asks.

"Yes," you whisper, your mouth dry.

"Speak up and let the court hear you."

Turn the page.

"Yes," you repeat. "She is. I've seen her cast her spells myself."

You are numb throughout the rest of your testimony. The verdict comes back as you knew it would—guilty. Your mother is sentenced to hang. She doesn't protest. She sacrificed her life so that you'll live and be able to care for James and Margaret. You only hope that you live your life in such a way to make her sacrifice worth it.

THE END

To follow another path, turn to page 11.
To read the conclusion, turn to page 101.

The next morning you meet with the magistrate. "I won't take the stand against my mother," you say. "She is no witch. And neither am I."

"Very well," says the magistrate. He leaves without another word.

Your trial is set for several weeks later. That morning you and your mother are led into the courthouse. Waiting for you is a group of three judges specially appointed by the governor. James and Margaret are sitting with one of your neighbors. Margaret is in tears. James looks bewildered.

The magistrates call witnesses. Some testify about your family's problems. Others tell of food spoiling or deformed animals being born. These are all the result of working against God, one magistrate argues. Mother then takes the stand.

Turn the page.

"Are you a witch?" asks the magistrate.

She looks at you and answers. "I am. But my son knew nothing of this. I am the only guilty one."

She is lying to protect you! You stand and shout, "No! It's not true!"

Nobody believes you. And nobody believes Mother either. "Should we take the word of an admitted witch?" the magistrate asks. "She's protecting the boy so he can carry on her evil ways!"

The court finds both you and your mother guilty and sentences you to death by hanging. You realize that you never had a chance in this trial. Times are hard and people need someone to blame. Unfortunately, that blame has been placed on you and your mother.

Accused witches weren't only women.
In Salem, six men were hanged for
witchcraft as well.

THE END

To follow another path, turn to page 11.
To read the conclusion, turn to page 101.

A few weeks later, the dreaded day comes. Your mother is to be hanged. You bring Margaret and James to the jail to say their good-byes. Then you send them home with a neighbor. They don't need to see this. But you will be there. You want Mother to have at least one supportive face in the crowd.

It is a cold day. A steady rain falls on the muddy ground. Mother is led to a wooden gallows. She does not struggle as a noose is fitted around her neck. You close your eyes at the final moment. You fall to your knees in the mud, trying to fight back tears.

You're filled with sadness and anger. Was there something more you could have done? Can you and the children stay here? It's the only home you've ever known. But the people here no longer feel like your friends and family.

You doubt that Abigail will even speak to you anymore. And even if she did, her parents will never allow you to court her. As far as the town is concerned, you're a witch's son.

With sadness, you realize that this is no longer your home. You don't know where you'll go. You just want to move as far from here as you can.

THE END

To follow another path, turn to page 11.
To read the conclusion, turn to page 101.

People who kept to themselves were often viewed with suspicion in colonial villages.

CHAPTER 4

LAYING BLAME

You're hungry. These days, you always feel hungry. The harvest was poor last fall. You and your family are just barely getting by. Life in Salem is difficult. It seems as if sickness and misery are around every corner.

You are walking home from church with your parents and four younger siblings. It is a cold, brisk day in February 1692. As you head to your small farm just outside of town, you notice something strange. A cloaked figure is moving alone in the distance.

"Who is that?" asks your sister Betsy.

Turn the page.

"That's none of our concern," your father answers sternly. But you can't help but look. The person seems to be looking right at you. A shiver runs down your spine. You wrap your thin cloak tighter around you. Suddenly the figure turns and darts off.

"Isn't that old Hannah?" your sister Mary asks. You're not sure, but you think she's right. Hannah is a poor widowed woman from town. She does not attend church and has always made you nervous.

When you arrive home, you are trembling. You're running a fever. But you feel ice cold. For several days, you are too sick to get out of bed. You toss and turn. You dream Hannah is hovering over you, laughing. You feel as if some dark magic has been used on you.

"I think old Hannah did something to me," you finally tell your mother. "I feel strange."

Your mother hesitates. She doesn't believe in the witchcraft accusations that have spread through Salem over the past weeks.

"Maybe we should talk to her," your mother says. "You can ask her yourself if she's done anything to you. I'll go with you."

The idea of confronting the old woman terrifies you. Who knows what she might do to you then?

➤ To speak with Hannah, turn to page **80**.

➤ To report her for witchcraft instead, turn to page **82**.

The next morning you are feeling better. You and your mother go into Salem. You knock on the door of Hannah's small home. No one answers. Just as you turn to leave, the door unlatches. Hannah opens it a crack, carefully looking outside.

"What!" she demands. "Why are you here?"

You take a step backward in alarm. But your mother places her hand firmly on your shoulder. There's no backing out now.

"I saw you outside of town the other day," you begin. You realize that you're not quite sure how to ask Hannah the question that's on your mind.

"What of it?" the old woman croaks.

"Well, I fell suddenly ill as soon as I saw you. Things have been strange here lately. I just wondered ..."

To your great surprise, Hannah throws back her head and laughs. It is a shrill and grating sound. It gives you the shivers once again.

"You got to thinking I might have cast a spell on you, is that it? Well I'm no witch, young lady."

"There, see?" your mother says. "Now let's hear no more of this."

Your mother apologizes to Hannah and takes you home. Still, you're not convinced. Should you forget about this or tell someone your suspicions?

→ *To report Hannah, turn to page 82.*

→ *To drop the matter, turn to page 84.*

You are afraid. You feel that you have to report your suspicions. The next day you go into town. You tell the Reverend Samuel Parris your story. He presses you for details. As you tell him what happened, you realize how silly it sounds.

"Accusing someone of witchcraft is serious business," Parris says. You can tell he does not really believe you. After all, your accusation is based on one illness and some dreams. Even in a village terrified of witchcraft, that's not enough to arrest someone.

But the idea of letting Hannah walk free scares you. If she finds out you reported her, she might take revenge. She could hurt you or your family.

You could tell Parris that you saw her chanting spells. It is not true, but it would probably be enough to convince him. You would have to lie, though. Is it worth it?

The Reverend Samuel Parris testified against several accused witches in Salem.

➸ To lie about seeing Hannah casting spells, turn to page **86**.

➸ To tell the truth, turn to page **89**.

You will respect your mother's wishes. Maybe your illness was just a coincidence. You're not even sure that the person you saw the other day was Hannah. Suspicion still gnaws at you. But you'll let it rest.

After a week you all but forget what happened. You're back to the struggle of day-to-day life. Your chores take up most of your time and energy.

A few days later, you hear the news that someone else has accused Hannah of witchcraft. A few girls from town claim that her spirit is haunting them. You know Hannah's accusers. Normally you wouldn't believe a word they say. But now you can't help but wonder.

You head to the church to find the Reverend Parris. You tell him your story.

Parris sighs. "We'll have to talk to the constable about this. And you'll have to testify if there's a trial," he says. "If there is witchcraft in this town, we must root it out. Tell the truth. If Hannah is innocent, God will save her."

Many accused witches were middle-aged or elderly women.

➻ To agree to testify, turn to page **91**.

➻ To refuse, turn to page **93**.

You hesitate for a moment, and then speak up. "I haven't told you the worst of it," you say. You go on to describe seeing Hannah dancing with the devil around a fire.

By the end of the tale, you're trembling with fear from the lie you've told. But Parris thinks you're afraid from remembering. You can tell he believes you. He sighs, nods slowly, and tells you that he'll speak with the constable.

Hannah is arrested the next day. You repeat your story to your parents, a magistrate, and others. You can tell by the look in your mother's eyes that she doesn't believe you.

That night you overhear your parents talking. "You know the girl is lying," Mother says. "Old Hannah is strange, but she's harmless."

Father sighs. "I agree that she's lying. But what can we do about it? She might accuse us next." You can't believe that you've made your parents afraid of you.

When Hannah's trial comes, you walk to the stand. At first you feel confident that you've done the right thing. After all, if Hannah is a witch, a small lie is worth putting her to justice. But as you swear before God to tell the truth, doubt creeps in. Suddenly, this all seems like a terrible mistake.

Magistrate John Hathorne asks you about what you've seen. You start with the truth. You speak of your sudden illness and the dreams in which Hannah haunted you. When the magistrate presses you for more, you pause.

Turn the page.

This is your last chance. You can tell the truth and risk letting Hannah go free. Or you can save your reputation by lying before God and the court.

Several accused witches were often tried on the same day.

⇥ *To go ahead with the lie, turn to page* **95**.

⇥ *To admit that you made up your story,*
turn to page **97**.

This is serious business. A woman's life hangs in the balance. The truth is the only course you should take.

The Reverend Parris gives you a long, hard look. You can tell he's wondering why you're here. "I understand your fears," he says finally. "These are strange times. Thank you for telling me this. God be with you."

You return home, knowing that at least you told the truth. Soon, the episode is all but forgotten. But a week later, you hear the news that someone else has accused Hannah of witchcraft. You feel a sense of dread. There will be a trial. After what you told the Reverend Parris, you know you'll be asked to testify.

Turn the page.

Alone, your story would not be enough to convict anyone. But as one of several witnesses, who knows what might happen?

➤ *To testify, go to page **91**.*

➤ *To refuse to take part in the trial, turn to page **93**.*

You agree to testify. After all, it isn't just about you anymore. The trial comes several weeks later. People crowd into the small courthouse. The panel of judges sits at a table, ready to hear the case. As you walk into the courthouse, your mother whispers in your ear. "I'm counting on you to speak the truth," she says sternly.

You watch as witnesses testify against Hannah. The girls tell the court that her spirit follows them. She is trying to turn them into witches, they say. Another witness says that Hannah bears the mark of the devil in her armpit. When the small red mark was pricked with a pin, it did not bleed. The crowd gasps, knowing this is proof of witchcraft.

Turn the page.

Finally, it's your turn. You tell your story. "I believe she cast a spell on me," you say. You glance at your mother. She looks both sad and disappointed.

You have mixed feelings when the verdict is read. Hannah is guilty. She is to be hanged. Part of you is glad that you helped put a witch to justice. But another part of you wonders if you might have been mistaken. You'll never be sure, but you did what you thought was right. You know your father will stand by you. You just hope you can win back your mother's trust as well.

THE END

To follow another path, turn to page 11.
To read the conclusion, turn to page 101.

You know that your parents would disapprove of you testifying against Hannah. And you really don't have any proof that she's done anything. People get sick all the time. You don't need witchcraft to explain that. And as for your dreams, they're hardly proof of anything.

"No, I don't think I have anything to say," you tell the minister. "All I really have is a feeling. Nobody should be hanged because of a feeling."

Parris looks at you carefully. "It's your choice to make," he says. "Let God be your guide. If this is what he is saying, you should listen."

Relief floods through you. You worried that Parris would think less of you for your decision. You thank him, say a short prayer, and run home.

Turn the page.

Hannah will still stand trial for witchcraft. Nothing you do could stop that. And you know there is a good chance she will be hanged. But you won't be a part of it. The Salem witch trials will go on, but they will go on without you.

THE END

To follow another path, turn to page 11.
To read the conclusion, turn to page 101.

You gulp. "I saw her do terrible things," you tell the court. "She stuck pins into dolls that look like people. She danced with the devil around a fire." You can feel Hannah's gaze on you as you speak. But you cannot meet it. You keep your head down and your voice soft. You repeat the lie one last time.

The rest of the trial is a blur. Magistrates call forth more witnesses. The judges reach a verdict. Hannah is guilty. She holds her head high as the verdict is read. You feel a pang of regret, but you dare not show it.

As you leave, your father takes you by the arm. But your mother leaves without speaking to you. She knows what you did. You don't think she'll ever understand it.

Turn the page.

A woman you believe to be a witch will hang.

But it has come at a great personal cost to you.

Was it worth it?

Nineteen people were hanged in Salem for witchcraft. One man was pressed to death with stones.

THE END

To follow another path, turn to page 11.
To read the conclusion, turn to page 101.

You break down in tears. It's all too much. You thought that lying would be the right thing. After all, you still think Hannah is a witch. But nothing is worth this horrible guilt you feel.

"I made it all up," you admit. The crowd erupts in confusion. "All I have is a bad feeling about Hannah and some nightmares."

You feel the anger of those gathered as you're led away. The case against Hannah has fallen apart, and the verdict quickly comes back. Hannah is not guilty of witchcraft.

As you leave the courthouse, people shake their heads at you, then look away. Timothy, a boy your age, glares at you. "Liar!" he spits before turning and walking away.

Turn the page.

Life will never be the same for you in Salem. You have lost the respect of your friends and neighbors. You know that your family will stand by you, but that is only a small consolation. You vow to spend the rest of your life making it up to Hannah and the rest of the town.

THE END

To follow another path, turn to page 11.
To read the conclusion, turn to page 101.

Puritans who lied and committed other sins sought forgiveness through prayer.

In Salem, 59 people were placed on trial for witchcraft.

CHAPTER 5

WHAT HAPPENED?

The Salem witch trials were a dark chapter in the history of Massachusetts. In all, 185 people were accused of witchcraft. Of these, 59 were tried and 31 were convicted. Nineteen were hanged. One man, Giles Corey, was pressed to death with stones after he refused to enter a plea. Most of the accused were women. Of the 31 people convicted, 25 were women.

It appears everything started with several young girls in Salem. They joined with a slave couple, Tituba and John Indian, to try to see their fortunes in a crystal ball made from an egg white dropped in a glass of water. This event may have fueled their imaginations. The girls started behaving in frightening ways—screaming, speaking gibberish, and contorting their bodies.

On February 29, 1692, three women were arrested. Sarah Good, Sarah Osborne, and Tituba were the first to be accused. The idea that witches were everywhere spread. Soon accusations were flying in Salem and throughout the Massachusetts Colony. Some of the accusations may have been pure mischief. Others could have been ways to settle grudges, and still others honest fears.

The trials were conducted in various courts in the area. The most famous trials were those held in Salem's Court of Oyer and Terminer, which is Latin for "Hear and Determine." Judges and magistrates in this court required very little evidence for a conviction. Many, including Sarah Good, were tried, convicted, and hanged. Others, such as Sarah Osborne, died in prison. Tituba spent three months in prison before being sold to a new owner.

It took months for public opinion to change about the witch trials. The Reverend Samuel Willard of Boston was outspoken in his criticism of the trials. Some suggested that his criticism might mean that he was really a witch, though no charges were ever brought against him.

The Reverend Increase Mather was a Puritan minister and a powerful figure in the government. He famously said, "It were better that 10 suspected witches should escape, than that one innocent person be condemned."

Massachusetts Governor William Phips agreed. Phips dissolved the Court of Oyer and Terminer on October 29, 1692. The Superior Court of Judicature replaced it. The new court placed much stricter rules on what kind of evidence would be allowed against the accused. As a result, convictions dropped sharply. In 1693 Phips pardoned all of the remaining people charged with witchcraft.

Even after the trials ended, people were still upset. The Puritan courts had acted improperly, people said. Even some of those involved in the trials agreed.

Several people who had served as jurors issued public apologies for their roles. The convictions were reversed in 1711. But for the executed, that decision came too late.

The Salem witch trials show us that our judicial system needs to be very careful in how it passes judgment. In U.S. courts today, prosecutors need firm evidence against anyone accused of a crime. It's true that some people are still falsely convicted, but treatment of the accused has greatly improved since those dark days of 1692.

Timeline

1692

January—Several girls in Salem, including the daughter of the Reverend Samuel Parris, become ill and begin acting strangely.

February—Doctors decide that the sick girls have been bewitched. The first three witchcraft accusations are made against the slave Tituba, Sarah Good, and Sarah Osborne; Tituba confesses to witchcraft. She spends three months in prison before being sold.

March–April—Many more people from Salem and other villages are accused of witchcraft.

May—Governor William Phips comes to Massachusetts from England.

106

June—Phips sets up the Court of Oyer and Terminer, with William Stoughton as the chief justice.

The witchcraft trials begin; Bridget Bishop is the first to be found guilty; she is hanged on June 10.

July 19—Sarah Good, Rebecca Nurse, and three other women are found guilty of witchcraft and hanged.

July–August—Many more women and men are tried, found guilty, and executed.

Sept. 19—Giles Corey is pressed to death for refusing a trial on charges of witchcraft; he is the only one of the accused to be killed without a conviction.

Sept. 22—Six women and two men are the last people executed in Salem for witchcraft.

October—Phips orders that unsubstantiated evidence no longer be allowed at the trials; on October 29 he dissolves the Court of Oyer and Terminer.

November—The Superior Court of Judicature is created to handle the remaining cases; the new standard for evidence results in only three convictions.

May 1693—Phips pardons everyone who still stands accused of witchcraft.

1697—The Reverend Samuel Parris leaves Salem.

1711—The Massachusetts government officially clears the names of all but five of the accused.

OTHER PATHS TO EXPLORE

In this book you've explored the events of the Salem witch trials. You've seen that it was a strange time, when fear and religious extremism drove people to accuse their neighbors of making deals with the devil.

Perspectives on history are as varied as the people who lived it. You can explore other paths on your own to learn more about what happened. Seeing history from many points of view is an important part of understanding it. Here are some other points of view to explore:

+ Judges had the final say in what happened to the accused. How might they have changed the way events unfolded?

+ Many of the people accused of witchcraft were poor. How did their position in society affect their fate?

+ Men in law enforcement were forced to carry out arrests of people they knew well. What would that have been like?

READ MORE

Burgan, Michael. *The Salem Witch Trials*. Minneapolis: Compass Point Books, 2005.

Hinds, Maurene J. *Witchcraft on Trial: From the Salem Witch Hunts to the Crucible*. Berkeley Heights, N.J.: Enslow Publishers, 2009.

Landau, Elaine. *Witness the Salem Witchcraft Trials with Elaine Landau*. Berkeley Heights, N.J.: Enslow Elementary, 2006.

Nardo, Don. *The Salem Witch Trials*. Detroit: Lucent Books, 2007.

INTERNET SITES

FactHound offers a safe, fun way to find Internet sites related to this book. All of the sites on FactHound have been researched by our staff.

Here's all you do:
Visit *www.facthound.com*
Type in this code: 9781429654784

GLOSSARY

constable (KON-stuh-buhl)—a police officer during colonial times

gallows (GAL-ohz)—a wooden frame used for hanging people convicted of crimes

indictment (in-DITE-muhnt)—an official charge against someone accused of committing a crime

Lord's Prayer (LORDZ PRAY-ur)—a prayer said by Christians; this prayer appears in the Bible

magistrate (MAJ-uh-strate)—a judicial officer who has the power to enforce the law

musket (MUHSS-kit)—a type of gun with a long barrel

Puritan (PYOOR-uh-tuhn)—a member of a strict Christian group common during the 1500s and 1600s

seizure (SEE-zhur)—a sudden loss of control over the brain or the body

testify (TESS-tuh-fye)—to state facts in court

verdict (VUR-dikt)—the decision on an issue in a court case

BIBLIOGRAPHY

The Salem Witchcraft Papers—1692 Salem Witch Trials: Documents and Participants. 27 Oct. 2010. http://etext.virginia.edu/salem/witchcraft/texts

Goss, K. David. *The Salem Witch Trials: A Reference Guide.* Westport, Conn.: Greenwood Press, 2008.

Hoffer, Peter Charles. *The Salem Witchcraft Trials: A Legal History.* Lawrence: University Press of Kansas, 1997.

Roach, Marilynne E. *The Salem Witch Trials: A Day-By-Day Chronicle of a Community Under Siege.* New York: Cooper Square Press, 2002.

Rosenthal, Bernard. *Salem Story: Reading the Witch Trials of 1692.* New York: Cambridge University Press, 1993.

Salem Witchcraft Trials 1692. 27 Oct. 2010. http://www.law.umkc.edu/faculty/projects/ftrials/salem/salem.htm

Index